Brief Immensity

poems by

Jeanine Stevens

Finishing Line Press
Georgetown, Kentucky

Brief Immensity

For Carol and Laverne Frith

ACKNOWLEDGMENTS

Grateful acknowledgement is made to the editors of the following journals
in which these poems first appeared.

Clare: "All Degrees of White."
Convergence: "Poetry 101," "Bodega Dunes."
Cosumnes River Journal: "Ode to Vernal Pools."
Dragonheart: "Mornings with Lying Snow."
Ekphrasis: "Haida Moon Mask," "Trade Goods," "To Georgia O'Keeffe,"
    "Composition," "Sunflowers."
Forge Poetry Journal: "Brief Immensity," "Potlatch."
Future Cycle Press: "The Sound of Snow."
Kind of Hurricane Press: "The Water Table."
Late Peaches—Poems by Sacramento Poets: "American Bittern."
Medusa's Kitchen: "Santa Ana Winds."
Poetalk: "Blue Taffeta."
Poetic Matrix: "Glacier at Land's End."
Poet's Espresso: "Dying at a Distance."
South Dakota Review: "V Shapes against Blue."
Squaw Valley Review: "Full of Sighs."
Tahoe Blues Anthology: "A Narrow Margin of Color."
Turtle Island Quarterly: "Minimums," "Channeled Wrack."
Winter Rising Anthology: "Sullivan's Pond."

Publisher: Leah Maines
Editor: Christen Kincaid
Cover Art: Gregory C. Chalpin
Author Photo: Gregory C. Chalpin
Cover Design: Elizabeth Maines

Printed in the USA on acid-free paper.
Order online: www.finishinglinepress.com
        also available on amazon.com

Author inquiries and mail orders:
Finishing Line Press
P. O. Box 1626
Georgetown, Kentucky 40324
U. S. A.

Table of Contents

Acorn clicking like a lunatic crystal,
A bud in loam, a time bomb full of forests.

The blue jay stabs at cracked corn. Sparrows follow.
Idiom of the beak, twelve nervous harpsichords.

David Young

All Degrees of White

Decision starts in first grade,
snow hugging trunks,
     trees barely visible.

We each receive a clear sheet,
not the acrid spongy manila,
but pure white smelling of ice,
and a blue or black crayon:
     no suggestions, no directions.

No sound, except roman numerals
ticking, a clanking water heater
wakened by wet mittens,
and the smell of warm wax in small hands.

Some begin right away: a dark glove,
parrot, wavy amoebic flakes, smokestack,
a lump of coal with sticks for eyes.
Others tear paper,
     created jagged waterfalls.

I think about small animals
hiding,
          choose blue.
My furry rabbit feet travel diagonally,
     disappear top right.

Haida Moon Mask

As he works, a distant flute soothes
the fretting child, sad because the moon

comes and goes. The father wants
to make something unmoving, unnamed.

Cedar gives up richness, hard and sweet.
Such a thick disk requires a strong hand.

An oval shape emerges, red cheeks,
and black quizzical eyebrows astonished

to be captured by chisel and adze. The child
murmurs, "ghost baby," and is happy.

A soft pile of golden shavings curl
at his feet. The father cleans his brush,

traces points in the sand—
imagines the next child startled by stars.

The Sound of Snow

At the bay window,
the first drift, cold enough
to stick. Some may hear snow
falling. I believe it.

Wet snow, lush like a kiss,
soon melts. Dry snow,
crisp as a harsh word, stays
on the ground, piles up
in berms, in dreams,
                in after-images.

I'm certain I hear flakes
cascade in a frenzy.

They told us no two
snowflakes are alike.

In reality, über-techno photos
report just a few basic patterns.

                      I think
the silence I hear is each searching
for its template, each starburst
seeking, finding, easing
into its parchment scented mate.

Sullivan's Pond

Decades ago, I circled frozen air.
The barricade upstream
collapsed. I moved
to the narrow slot, ducked under
the footbridge, the ice un-groomed, pebbly.
Summer willows bent and hooked,
created snags on the surface, like eyelets
ready to fasten errant skaters.
The ice appeared thick.
If I fell through
no one would find me until spring.
They would all be sorry,
wouldn't have to tolerate
my fidgeting, my gawkiness,
my breezy thoughts.
I wanted to keep on, maybe north
to Duluth, find a new family.
A downed tree blocked my path.
A scarlet cardinal, the only
color, fastened legs tight
to a spur, tilted his head,
and scolded me back
to the warming hut and frothy cocoa.
Now I wonder, how many
other times I've tested myself,
if it is true that *willows*
*never forget how to be young?**

*Quote, William Stafford

A Narrow Margin of Color
South Lake Tahoe, January

At 6,000 feet, star scented air,
the moon wears her large ring
—translucent, ocular fuzz.
We step out at midnight—
a monochromatic nocturne
in an azure tinged sky.
We admire the Tamarack's black trunk
and red twigged dogwood.

A glacial spectrum.
I think moongarten.

Next day, on snowshoes,
we trek the meadow, sun so bright,
a quick stop to rest our eyes.
There in deep shade,
a neon that disappears in bright sun.
You say, "It's the water content
that makes the crystals seem
electrified, a filament lit from within."

I've seen the sign above small taverns,
a martini glass with an olive just-that-blue,
and on paint chips: *Feather Falls,*
Peace River, June Lake, Carthage…
but the closest I come—Chagall's pencil,
writing the sky over Vitebsk.

V Shapes against Blue

In this withering light, three slender oaks
expose their imperfections,
do not ask to be noticed.
Like Macbeth's hags, they clump,
intertwine spindly branches in dry mud.

Unashamed, they flaunt warts, cankers,
black galls full of fungi.
Pests suck sage colored limbs,
knobs disfigure brittle ribs.
Yet they accept,
                    even tolerate my looking.

Their upper limbs toss
so many V shapes in a sullen sky.
I want to think violet or vermilion,
hues that belong below ground
where glassy bugs gnaw, rearrange roots.
I want a side view: a slice of earth
to see pink worms and purple voles.

Come spring, I don't know
if they will sprout lime colored leaves
graced with copper finches.
These woods seem an unbreathing place,
birds barely here: their songs
elude me. I grow even paler
                    in winter's deep shade.

The Water Table

November, the metal roof should be graced
with heavy frost,
          the needed storm only paltry.
Not an arborist, but I think ground water
sinks dangerously low.

Which direction are the roots taking, so devoid
of moisture in yet another drought year?
Will they seek horizontal,
or tendril down hungrily gnawing
          to open pockets that hold nothing, voids
confused as everyone else?

I think of the pot-bound pink lemon you just planted
in deep earth, roots a tough spiral,
like a tightly woven basket,
          except
for one green stubborn shoot fingering
down through the ceramic hole—
seeking life. Reminds me of Dylan Thomas:

> *Force that through the green fuse*
> *drives the flower.*

What if I've been planted in the wrong place
at the wrong time, wrong latitude, wrong century?

Trade Goods
Inspired by a sketch—Sydney Prior Hall, 1881
The Sioux Buffalo Dance, Fort Qu'Appelle

I am ten, looking at a museum sketch.
I'm puzzled by so few, only four
dancers in costume framed
by glass windows and picket fences.
Massive curly heads stomp and snort,
faces hidden in prairie-green paint.
The Mounties relax long muskets.

Old chiefs stand attentive in wrapped blankets.
One wears a black top hat
with two crinkled eagle feathers,
too delicate for travel, but he won't be going far.

He sees no wrong in owning this hat.
Perhaps he can trade his worn blanket
for the matching jacket, vest,
and golden watch fob. He is brought back
to the dance—*Tatanwacipi.*

So many riches: horns, hair, ribs, and tails
to fabricate rattles, ropes, sleds and brushes
—the buffalo, a utility unto itself.

He remembers how they struggled
in drifting snow and fast running streams,
immobilized, so easy to pluck off.

Mornings with Lying Snow:
The Scottish Highlands

January in the Sierras.
I open a discard from the local library,
The British Isles, by G. H Dury and a map
recording weather patterns
in the otherworldly Grampian Mountains.
Here deeply grooved glacial troughs
and wide-stream valleys
cradle snow throughout the year.

I'm struck by the ink-black illustration.
Ovals, like dark wax under
a royal seal, mark the drumlins,
forecasting frequent clouds and obscure sun.

It's not the map, or the way the cartographer
drops a line that holds me,
but the enchantment of words. Lucky
the person, even in summer, who steps out
with the task of recording:
"Mornings with lying snow."

Ode to Vernal Pools

I praise whatever formula, caldron,
that factory somewhere with bellowing silk,
shooting phosphorous,
indigo, calcite, sulfur skyward to settle
in this inverted bowl each spring,
gushing with lime green rainwater,
brim overflowing.
Bloom-filled rings appear in water's place,
ooze elfin carpets
of meadowfoam, downingia and goldfields.

Each a unique shape these petals,
perhaps ancient cousins to dahlia, peony, violet,
or even kin to archaic garlands:
cornflowers and hollyhocks
strewn across hearts
of the first human graves.
You are a homeland,
the brilliance of everyday things,
a trust written in the world's oldest ledgers.

Small girls in berets and vests peep
over your rim, gaze at magic rings glistening,
as if lit from underneath
by white florescence.
These girls fall silent, do not ask
or wonder who hibernates, incubates,
reseeds, cradles these lovelies.

I'm overjoyed as translucent,
baby-faced, fairy shrimp
reappear, swim on their backs,
seem to smile— and practice winking.

Channeled Wrack

~after Rachel Carson, The Edge of the Sea. 1955

A weed of low growth,
first of sea plants to colonize the shore.

Three-fourths of its life on land,
yet a true seaweed, basic orange, basic brown,
a symbol of the ocean's threshold.

Earth's most ancient plant,
the Greek name for dusky, thrives
in dim and shadowed places.

An evolutionary success story.

On the flood tide, starfish move up,
tumble on tiptoes
emerge from these great meadows of the sea.

Blue Taffeta

A thrill at low tide when moon rises,
re-claims her basin and drinks mightily
from deep depressions.

Along the shore, a seascape reminiscent
of O'Keeffe: descending horizontals,
rose sand, simple wave, inked sky
and one bright pinhole on the horizon.

Much like a nocturnal story board, add
what you like: a lost city, porches, balustrades
and pungent shore holly on biscuit-size dunes

where miniscule inhabitants scurry
with red thimbles to gather the last light
before the next swell.

Georgia knew what she was doing,
arranged a template where I scaffold
my own version of low tide:
moonglow, nocturnal, delicious and shaggy,

the whoosh of blue taffeta
at midnight, off-tempo tango in ¾ time,
remnants of golden ambergris.

Bodega Dunes

At the end of June, a small girl constructs Stonehenge
out of driftwood, then buries her parents.
Two boys plant adult-size shovels in the sand,
an American Gothic stark on the horizon.
Most doze under bright quilts. Sound doesn't carry,
any disagreements broken by rushing surf,
picked up by wind, then dropped next to someone's
Sunday Chronicle, brie and beer.
On this far coast, I join in their sleeping,
this wanting platform cantilevered
out at the end of the world. We are unconscious,
drifting in watery dreams. We are relieved
when Dads finally wake, help children hoist bird,
flower, and flag kites in a long Pacific sky.

Brief Immensity

In late May, we don't expect
such sweet moisture, insistent droplets
streaking the skylight.
On the freshly tilled hillock,
new bedding plants drench in green rain.
We are grateful for this respite
before summer heat brings
blooming immensity, prairie
coneflowers and heirloom zinnias.
By July, insistent delta breezes
give relief; we open windows,
sheets tucked so tight you can bounce
a coin on the surface.
We want to be the first man
and woman who stood and scanned
the next berm, the lunar sky.
Staying up late, we gaze at the mystical
reconnaissance much as the lone deer rises
in a fern meadow and pauses,
nose to the horizon, wet,
vegetative eyes glossed at the kind
of light that halts and waits for other things
to begin, something beyond, before
returning to her thicket,
here and now—animal peace.

Glacier at Land's End

Under dazzling clouds,
Dall sheep, muscular and sure-footed
perch on sharp shale.

Our truck rattles across the suspension bridge,
wood slats clattering,
brown feathered grouse scattering,
the river a milky wash.

Noon melt, too late for hiking the Matanuska.
We go anyway,
leave the doors unlocked.

In a crevice, we see where wind and sun wore
this ancient ice down to a steep hole,
aquamarine crystals like spun glass hold archaic air.
Even birds know better than to roost here.

The outward path meanders, obscured.
The glint of glacial water
hardens, glistens slick and frigid.

The arctic sun gives faint light,
ice whistles and creaks. We cannot find
our way, not certain if we are advancing or retreating.
The sea is not far, but has other worries.

Looking back, I notice the sheep
have grown larger.
They are the slate gray clouds floating,
and have no feet.

Sunflowers

~a Painting, Vincent van Gogh

You would have to be walking here
   to find them, dumped among shriveled fescue

and brown tick weed, features plucked
   clean. The once golden manes, wet-veined

and plush, stiffen: bleached centers suck in.
   Their coarse, pock-marked faces glower

at the sky: hooked noses, sunken eyes, pits
   and shadows, angry as Iroquois husk masks.

They do not rest, but reach and thrust
   an after-image, parchment stars spinning

in blackness, heat grown cold, sweet oil
   drained away. They will be tilled in spring,

the disk edge grinding fibers into fodder,
   nourishing yet another field shot with yellow.

American Bittern

A dark eye swivels.
If I had looked away
just before, I would
have missed speckled wedges,
chips like a Klimt painting:
bronze, ochre and lime green
spliced among cattails.
My eye struggles to keep up
with this fleeting image
like imprinting a memory:
attention-selection-retrieval.
Just a hint, a piece
to build that fear again,
the dark alleyway,
pebbles rattling
deep cracks in the center,
an overused worry stone.
Or the eye chart, a click
of the lens: blur, fuzz,
which memory is
correct, A or B?
Which is better, B or A?
When I leave that thought,
the bittern suddenly thrusts
a slow beak to the sky,
becomes a vertical shaft,
one with the reeds, invisible.
November grasses in still water
barely move. Harlequin shapes
dissolve my blinker's moment.

To Georgia O'Keeffe
~a Photo, Ansel Adams

The burned out stump, an obelisk filling the gray sky,
magnifies visions of Calla's centering seeds,
Canna's gaping throat.

This high alpine forest suits you, wrapped
in a dusky cloak, a diminutive form
folded into Sequoia's shattered bark.

So far from your wet lakes and pale sun,
we might think you merely resting, but here is room
to slip inside the shaggy trunk,
contemplate higher clouds, pointed pines.

In the distance, dun-colored earth, and even
the small brown lizard glows light and dark.
You don't brush away the earth that clings to your hem—
matter out of place, but keep it with you.

Dying at a Distance

A low moan, vapor tracks
crease the Coast Range:
    whitish columns, fuzzy

looping lines mimic
    cirrocumulus clouds

then shape oval stepping-stones
    across the crimson sky.

Shasta Indians say souls
leave the body *before* death,
    you can see footsteps

    in the atmosphere
those who are
    "Dying at a distance."

When I think
of all the manmade vapors
    crossing our heavens,

I see entire civilizations
    simply walking away.

The Celadon Bird
Indianapolis, October

Early morning walk at Monument Circle.
Few sounds, horse and carriage at rest.

A tiny bird sits on the dark pavement,   *only 4 inches*
a striking shade like rich damask.

Eyes closed, I consider nudging him
with my camera but fear he may topple.   *never stirred*

A clear and bright day, but mist to him,
so quiet with opaque lids. So still,   *the end of days*

like a meditation, not moving this small
green heart. Feathers, a brilliance that could
be found in Costa Rica. Maybe a warbler up

from Tennessee. I think he may be dying.   *no winter song*
He will not run back and forth like a sandpiper.

He does not move just thinking: *unaware of danger*
nothing, nothing, nothing.

No glance anywhere; I do not want
to leave him, but I a traveler,
have no child's soft shoe box for rescue.   *bower*

As I watch, one eye opens.
What does he see? Shiny Florsheims
clicking along, or the flower cart's
red wheels running round and round?

I have no further thoughts and walk on.
Later in the day, returning at half-past four   cycle

from lunch at the grand Athenaeum
and the Vonnegut Memorial Library,

autumn sun gleams just enough to grace
the Soldier's and Sailor's Monument.

Little pilgrim—gone, perhaps removed   *taken*
by a local to an alleyway close by.

In his place a bright spot of yellow satin
and thin shadow of the angel
who perches on top the observation tower.

Poetry 101

~A Cento

I am writing this poem on the back
of a grocery list. In the opening words this:
"Too many stars for our own good."

Empty places of the poem:
arms lopped, something dragged away:
the odor of the poem.

This is what I see in my dreams about final exams,
a bulletin from the poetry factory:
We like our images stuck on with morticians wax.

(You can't repeat this class in summer:
the course is only offered once.)

The truth is none of my relatives writes poems.

A little poem, a sigh, at the cost
of indescribable losses:
fingerprints of the universe, maps you cannot read.

****

Ruth Stone: "Theology," "Body Among Trees," "Orange Poem Praising Brown," "Flash," "This Space."

Wislawa Szymborska: "Evaluation of an Unwritten Poem," "Brueghel's Two Monkeys," "Nothing Twice," "In Praise of my Sister," "A Large Number."

Minimums

In the foothills, a slender pine is the perfect transition,
the oval owl sleeps secure in a round hole on the bluff,

and somewhere, a flock of five pointed stars exist
just as I have imagined. In human thought there are no

minimums. What seems a void is rapidly filled like soft air
packed in Vermeer's white pitcher. Always, a decision:

shorten the fugue, omit the tree from the pencil sketch,
take the elbow out of the poem, the raisins from the pudding.

The ax handle explains the history of tools. Fossil grains
prove the origin of beans. Even Haiku gives us an entire season.

In the labyrinth of cave, the mind dreams on walls and
a slim finger begins our moonlit history in a single night.

Santa Ana Winds

In October, raging gusts charge in
                 from the Mojave.
Some students excused from school,
fight the fiery ring surrounding the Valley.

Embers smolder
all through Thanksgiving
when holiday garlands already crisscross
the intersection of Sherman Way
and Canoga Avenue, a silver bell
swaying in the center.

From our window, Mother wraps
the last gift, thinks about Wisconsin,
watches blistering gales return
stripping young banana leaves.

I walk to town, sagging tinsel hangs
shredded and limp
                 from thick wires.

Composition
~a Painting, Vasily Kandinsky

Off-color rainbow,
magenta, spruce and slate,
caps the inked heart,
    a heart in motion.

Black stick eyes,
or are they stitched—deft lashes
blink right and left,
   a warrior's headdress.

A limpet's foot
drags a kite tail through amber canyons.

Art that is a mountain,
low burning creosote, mute scarlet
     splitting stones.

A slight smear, background sun
sweeps star shadows,
    a tale to tell.

In the shade, a painted desert,
something of Arizona: Navaho.

The heart that is
     a heart that holds.

Dungeness

We stopped at the wharf,
bought two large cooked crabs,
sunset orange shells with smears of red.
Carried to a worn table, we each
grabbed a claw, pulling out triangles
of sweetness. Our lips turned oily
from butter that began in our mouths then slathered
down arms, so slick we could hardly hold
the bottle of chilled Chardonnay.
Salt spray softened the sour dough bread we tore
into chunks, as if we had never eaten—
as if this was our first meal on earth.
We moved on to meaty bodies, fringed
membranes no barrier. Fingers were pink and raw
with moisture and small cuts from sharp shards.
Hesitating, much as an animal looks
up from his kill, I closed my eyes, heard
the sea wall whisper, tasted
the Pacific on my tongue. You cut the lemon
in half, juice spattered my face. Startled,
I decided I loved the word crustacean,
then noticed a warning sign: Lyme Disease.
Too busy to care, not even time for a photo,
other problems easily put on hold.
Day darkened, sopped paper plates
collapsed. The last fragment finished,
jeweled remnants piled in our wake.

Manhattan

Evening, early January,
the drink deep and straight up
with crimson cherry,
slow sips while we anticipate
menu selections: prime rib, lobster
or the fisherman's platter
with this person
so close to me for 30 years.
We enjoy the privacy of dark booths,
tables laminated with nautical maps and coins.
Other twosomes, faces in the glow
of cell phones ignore each other.
A slow start to the day,
two hours in bed with the Chronicle,
considering the annual white sales.
Time spent on nothing really,
the last wreath and bell stored away,
remembering children
who came caroling on the 26th
"To make the season last," they said.
Over creamy chowder,
I look up to a painting of a dog
in a sailor suit smoking a pipe
and another of Johnny Depp as Jack Sparrow.
Some wouldn't consider this place
romantic, just a throwback.
You like sweets.
I give you the maraschino.

In Situ

Why is there under that poem, always an-other poem?
Lucille Clifton

Go easy with the initial scratching

first mouth=cave/	first anchor=tree
first wound=sap/	first core=garnet
first path=spore/	first star=opal.

Salvage archeologists meet deadlines for the next overpass.
Bulldozers expose Miwok elders dangling from Valley strata.

At the base of the Pyrenees, the anxious and eager
lopped off one breast from the ivory Venus
content in her grotto 14,000 years.

Here is a poem in place, situated boldly on the surface,
gently lift and use, lily bright, circular flat,
all contained. Thoughts

excavated in denser layers need patience.
Then we know we've touched something rare.

The fragmented basket pulled from the banks
of the North Yuba, requires the delicacy of airbrush
to dislodge roots
          to find the unaltered word-bed.

A dozing bird holds a stone in one foot to awaken
her sleeping eye. Stone within the root.

The midden so rich and unending.
If lucky, even today, I can reach
    the bone-laden tar,
        the other poem,
            the first translucent star.

(In situ. Items found undisturbed, in their original location, as in the earth.)

Full of Sighs

On Interstate 5, I pull north near the Coast Range
enveloped in a strong scent of pet bear.
From an oak forest, the green man emerges.
I have fantasized his bristles, felt wrapped
in the tight blown faces of his bindweed.
How fetching the bit of beaver fat
in his beard, brown berry eyes flecked gold,
a slow swagger, a smolder about him.
On his back, a rage of scars. I bask
in his vermillion coals,
juniper pods so old they've turned to gin.
I don't care how decrepit—
myths are hard work!
Just for a moment he gives
me a break from rubber and asphalt.
Foothills gleam orchid, twilight softens vastness.
Sharp edges of the highway push day into night,
the Pacific full of sighs: waves waffle
in black, endless, undulating weaves.

Forecast: the sea, calm and rippled.
This is my life.

Potlatch
~after the Kwakiutl

Begin by giving away $10 packs of cigarettes,
copper chafing dishes, doilies and anamacasters,
Schaeffer ink pens, milk pitchers, travel brochures,
potato chips and cracklings.

Have everyone give away manual can openers,
polka dot bow ties, menus for the Brown Derby,
fitted bed sheets, etched goblets, dusty packs
of Walnettos, jars of Nescafé and slot machines.

Pretend to be a queen. Have the men pretend
to be ornaments and walking sticks. Have the
women pretend to be chefs and refrigerator magnets.

Talk Siberian or another language. Put a limbo pole
at the front door so people have to dance low to enter.
Hang cans of Chef Boyardee spaghetti and a
ball cap collection on the pole. Conduct a raffle.
Add shoe horns and pickle forks— make a small racket.

Give away foil balls from cream cheese wrappers.
Give everyone a new name from the bird world.
Go and look again: maybe Snap-On-tools, straight-
edged razors, psychedelic bed rolls, "Happy Days"
lunch box and skunk traps? Have an auction.

A Sacramento poet by way of Indiana, Jeanine Stevens is the author of two poetry books: *Inheritor*, Future Cycle Press and *Sailing on Milkweed* (a finalist for the ABZ First Book Prize), published by Cherry Grove Collections. Tiger's Eye Press released her latest chapbook, *Needle in the Sea*. She has other chapbooks from Poets Corner Press, Indian Heritage Council, Green Fuse Poetic Arts and Rattlesnake Press.

Jeanine has won poetry awards from the MacGuffin Poet Hunt, the Stockton Arts Commission, *Ekphrasis*, The Bay Area Poet's Coalition, Mendocino Coast Writer's Conference, WOMR Cape Cod Community Radio and was one of two finalists for the William Stafford Award. She has four Pushcart Nominations.

Her poems have appeared in T*he Evansville Review, Tipton Poetry Journal, Verse Wisconsin, Arsenic Lobster, Perfume River, Clackamas Literary Review, Forge Poetry Journal, Pearl, Cider Press Review, Rosebud, Penumbra, Edge, Centrifugal Eye, Stoneboat* and *North Dakota Review.*

Instructor at American River College for thirty two years, she taught courses in Anthropology, Women's Studies and Psychology. Jeanine also edited newsletters for the California Postsecondary Education Commission and the California Department of Transportation. Besides writing, she also enjoys Romanian folk dance and collage. Many of her art pieces have illustrated her poems and chapbooks and have been exhibited at Red Dot Gallery, DaDas Art Gallery and the Sacramento Poetry Center.

www.ingramcontent.com/pod-product-compliance
Lightning Source LLC
LaVergne TN
LVHW051610080426
835510LV00020B/3224